EARLY AMERICAN DESIGN MOTIFS

SUZANNE E. CHAPM...

Second Revised & Enlarged Edition

DOVER PUBLICATIONS, INC.,
NEW YORK

Published in Canada by General Publishing
Company, Ltd., 30 Lesmill Road, Don Mills,
Toronto, Ontario.
Published in the United Kingdom by Con-
stable and Company, Ltd., 10 Orange Street,
London WC 2.

This Dover edition, first published in 1974, is
a revised and greatly expanded version of the
work first published in 1952 by Dover Publications, Inc.

DOVER *Pictorial Archive* SERIES

International Standard Book Numbers
(Clothbound): 0-486-23084-8
(Paperbound): 0-486-22985-8
Library of Congress Catalog Card Number: 73-86040

Manufactured in the United States of America
Dover Publications, Inc.
180 Varick Street
New York, N.Y. 10014

INTRODUCTION

The basic principles of design are alike the world over. From the earliest times the same simple motifs have been used by man to decorate his creations and possessions; namely, the straight line, wavy, zig-zag line, circle, half-circle, spiral, and the S-curve. We find these motifs with their many variations used singly or in combination over and over again. The illustrations in this book bear out this fact.

These early American motifs have all the charm of their German, Dutch, English, and French origin, for the same traditions were carried on in this country, and these motifs were inspired by the same common objects of everyday life: birds, animals, fish, trees, flowers, and human figures.

The bird forms used in early American decoration are many and varied. Let us mention a few. Two small birds contemplate a cherry (Fig. 284). A peacock preens his feathers (Fig. 355). Cocks' heads combine to form decorative motifs on hinges (Figs. 471 and 478). A sloe-eyed bird crouches amidst fruit and flowers (Fig. 52). Another peacock surveys his domain from the top of a carnation and lily plant (Fig. 154). A double-headed dove and preening peacock combine on a Pennsylvania German pottery plate to form a beautiful design (Fig. 356). The Distelfink, standing in realistic fashion upon a flowering branch and plucking its breast to feed its young with its own blood (Fig. 362), forms a fine composition on a pie dish of Pennsylvania German colored slip ware. Cocks on wrought iron weather vanes (Figs. 328, 329, 333, 334); carved and painted toy birds (Figs. 338–340, 343); and a handsome carved wooden rooster with a marvelous tail (Fig. 337) might each be inspiration for a woodcut or an embroidery worked in simple stitches.

The heart in combination with flowers and birds decorates pottery, furniture, embroideries, and many everyday articles. In the embroidered border of a petticoat made in 1714 large heart-shaped "flowers" hang from the branches of a tree (Fig. 317). Four hearts form a simple decorative motif for the center of an appliqué design (Fig. 20), then recur as the center of a stencil design (Fig. 88) and again as the wrought iron hasp from a Conestoga wagon box (Fig. 476). In the designs of the double-headed dove, the body of the bird is drawn in the shape of a heart (Figs. 131, 356, 361).

Fanciful fruit and flowering trees are another favorite motif, one which may have been inspired by the printed cottons brought from India. Figures 306, 311, 313–318 show a few examples of such trees, and Figures 201, 202, 277, 279 seem especially to show the influence of printed India cottons. These designs do not reproduce nature in a realistic manner, but, rather, they are a straightforward approach to the medium in which they were worked. Crewel embroidery is a very popular form of creative work today; and we hope that these motifs, many of which have never been reproduced before, will be an inspiration to present-day designers of embroidery and printed textiles.

The tulip was one of the principal decorative symbols of the Pennsylvania Germans and may be found in great variety on their pottery and other utensils. Often the tulip is combined with asters, fuchsias, birds, fish, and human figures. Particularly well done designs are shown in Figures 90, 93, 125 and 355.

Stencils, being quick and easy, were useful in decorating furniture, walls and floors. A large variety of these stencil designs has been included in this book.

Figures 146, 148–150, 436 are designs from a carved chest made in Salem, Massachusetts, in 1796. These designs might be enlarged to make stencils for use on trays and furniture.

The beautifully etched and enamelled glass made in Pennsylvania by the craftsmen who worked for Henry William Stiegel give us five lovely motifs (Figs. 107, 108, 116, 128).

To the inventiveness of the blacksmith we owe not only ordinary household necessities but also forged, or wrought ironwork such as latches, hinges, fences, and decorative balconies, gates and furniture hardware. Figures 452–461, 463, 465 are a few examples from fence standards, and Figures 462, 464, 466–497 from hinges and hasps.

The student can gain inspiration from early American motifs if he studies them with the intention of using their best qualities. In rendering these motifs in black and white and with the greatest economy of line, the quality of design and composition—the spirit and character of the creators—is brought out clearly. In this book the illustrator has endeavored to give some idea of this quality by the use of black in each individual motif.

A more complete discussion of the historical background of these motifs may be found in the books listed in the Bibliography.

For encouragement and help in gathering together the material for this book, the author wishes to express her sincere thanks to Mr. Russell H. Kettell, and to the members of the staff of the Boston Museum of Fine Arts: Mr. Larry Salmon, Curator of the Department of Textiles; Miss Gertrude Townsend, Curator Emeritus of the Department of Textiles; Miss Elizabeth Reigal, Supervisor of Sales; Mrs. Yves Henry Buhler, Research Fellow in the Department of American Decorative Arts. The author is also indebted to Mrs. Celia Vandermark Scudder, Mrs. Marjorie Childs Hunt, Mr. Richard B. K. McLanathan and Mr. Bernard V. Bothmer.

The author is most grateful to Miss Karol A. Schmiegel, Assistant Registrar of The Henry Francis du Pont Winterthur Museum, for sending her the photographs of the bedspread and wall hangings in the Winterthur collection and especially to Miss Gayne Evans, Registrar, for permission to use the motifs from these beautiful pieces for this book.

SUZANNE E. CHAPMAN

Lexington, Massachusetts
February, 1974

CONTENTS

List of Motifs and Sources vi

Bibliography xix

Index of Motifs According to Original Use xx

I. Florals *(Motifs 1 through 293)* 1

II. Landscapes *(Motifs 294 through 327)* 84

III. Birds and Animals *(Motifs 328 through 407)* 104

IV. Borders *(Motifs 408 through 437)* 122

V. Miscellaneous 128

    Alphabets *(Motifs 438 through 442)* 128

    Geometrics *(Motifs 443 through 451)* 131

    Historical Metalwork *(Motifs 452 through 497)* 133

LIST OF MOTIFS AND SOURCES

COLOR ILLUSTRATIONS
(follow page 12)

A. Toleware teapot, late 18th century.

B. Painted wooden box.

C. Painted wooden chest.

D. Red earthenware sgraffito plate, Pennsylvania, c. 1800. *New-York Historical Society.*

E. Painted chest, probably from Pennsylvania.

F. Detail of chest, probably from Pennsylvania, late 18th century.

G. Appliqué quilt, made by Mrs. Quigley, Virginia, 1853.

H. Patchwork and appliqué quilt, made by Ella Butler, Staten Island, New York, c. 1810.

I. Appliqué quilted coverlet, Long Island, New York, 1842. Collection Mrs. Charles Ingalls.

J. Appliqué quilt, California, late 19th century. *M. H. de Young Memorial Museum,* San Francisco.

K. Linen coverlet, made by J. Wirick, St. Paris, Ohio, 1850.

L. Patchwork and appliqué quilted bedspread.

M. Blue and white coverlet, St. Clairsville, Ohio, c. 1840.

N. Gray stoneware jar, made by Jacob Caire, Poughkeepsie, New York, c. 1852.

O. Gray stoneware jar, made by J. Fisher, Lyons, New York, c. 1878.

P. Gray stoneware jar, made by N. Clark & Co., Lyons, New York, mid-19th century.

Q. Gray-tan stoneware jug, made by I. Seymour, Troy, New York, mid-19th century.

BLACK AND WHITE ILLUSTRATIONS

I. Floral Motifs

1, 2. White quilted chair covers. *Museum of Fine Arts*, Boston. Acc. Nos. 23.7, 23.10*

3. Embroidered quilt by Cynthia Arnsworth, late 18th century. *Philadelphia Museum of Art.*

4. Appliqué quilt, Ohio, c. 1820.

5. Quilted cushion. *Museum of Fine Arts*, Boston. Acc. No. 23.5.

6. Embroidered quilt, Haverhill, Massachusetts. Courtesy Old Sturbridge Village.

*Reference designations according to Boston Museum of Fine Arts Catalog system.

7. Quilt with "Pumpkin Blossom" pattern. *Art Institute of Chicago.*
8, 9. Tufted and patchwork quilt made by Sarah Parell, 1826.
10, 11. Appliqué quilt, Baltimore, Maryland, 1815. *Brooklyn Museum.*
12. Tufted and patchwork quilt made by Sarah Parell, 1826.
13. Tufted and patchwork quilt made by Sarah Parell, 1826.
14. Appliqué quilt, "Martha's Vineyard" pattern.
15. Tufted and patchwork quilt made by Sarah Parell, 1826.
16. Appliqué quilt, "Lily" pattern, 1835.
17. Quilt, "Oriental Poppy" pattern. *Art Institute of Chicago.*
18. Appliqué quilt, "North Carolina" or "Virginia Lily" pattern, 1840.
19. Appliqué quilt, Maine, 1840.
20. Quilt, "Leaf and Heart" pattern, 19th century.
21. "Album" or "Friendship" quilt, New Jersey, middle of 19th century.
22, 23. Appliqué quilt, 19th century.
24, 25. Appliqué quilt made by Mary Rosalie Presstman Myers in Baltimore, Maryland, 1815. *Brooklyn Museum.*
26. Appliqué quilt in "Poinsettia" pattern, 1850. *The Art Institute of Chicago.*
27. Appliqué "Circuit Rider" quilt, 1862.
28. Appliqué quilt, made by Mary Rosalie Presstman Myers in Baltimore, Maryland, 1815. *Brooklyn Museum.*
29. Appliqué quilt, made for the Carpenter family, Harrison, New York, 1852.
30. Appliqué "Circuit Rider" quilt, 1862.
31. Appliqué quilt made for the Carpenter family, Harrison, New York, 1852.
32. Appliqué "Circuit Rider" quilt, 1862.
33. Appliqué quilt made for the Carpenter family, Harrison, New York, 1852.
34–36. Appliqué "Circuit Rider" quilt, 1862.
37. Appliqué quilt made for the Carpenter family, Harrison, New York, 1852.
38. Appliqué quilt, "Rose" pattern, 19th century. *Brooklyn Museum.*
39. Appliqué quilt made for the Carpenter family, Harrison, New York, 1852.
40. Stencil. *Metropolitan Museum of Art*, New York.
41. Floor stencil, Dorchester, Massachusetts, c. 1825. *Society for the Preservation of New England Antiquities*, Boston.
42, 43. Stencils. *Metropolitan Museum of Art*, New York.
44–48. Stencils. *Metropolitan Museum of Art*, New York.
49. Wall stencil, Josiah Sage house, South Sandisfield, Massachusetts.
50. Wall stencil, David Baldwin house, New Marlborough, Massachusetts.
51. Stencil on overmantel, Josiah Sage house, South Sandisfield, Massachusetts.
52. Pennsylvania German chair stencil. *Philadelphia Museum of Art.*
53. Stencil, "Fruit Dish" motif, probably by Moses Eaton.
54. Wall stencil, Josiah Sage House, South Sandisfield, Massachusetts.
55. Stencil from parlor overmantel and panel, Salmon Wood house, Hancock, New Hampshire.
56. Wall stencil by Moses Eaton, Ezekiel Hanson house, South Windham, Maine, first quarter 19th century.
57. Wall stencil by Moses Eaton, Sr. from house near Hancock, New Hampshire, 19th century. Owned by the Wilfred Westons.

58. Floor stencil, Joseph Lynde house, Melrose, Massachusetts.
59, 60. Wall stencil by Moses Eaton from a house in Lyman, first quarter 19th century. Owned by the Maine Historical Society.
61. Wall stencil by Moses Eaton, Sr. from house near Hancock, New Hampshire, 19th century. Owned by the Wilfred Westons.
62. Appliqué quilt, "Princess Feather" pattern.
63. Appliqué quilt, "Fern" pattern, made by Mary Wellman Eshelman, Red Haw, Wayne County, Ohio, c. 1780.
64. Wall stencil by Moses Eaton, Sr. from house near Hancock, New Hampshire, 19th century. Owned by the Wilfred Westons.
65. Wall stencil, Ebenezer Robinson house, South Reading, Vermont.
66. Floor stencil, Ebenezer Waters house, West Sutton, Massachusetts. Owned by Dr. John W. Tuttle.
67. Wall stencil, Ebenezer Robinson house, South Reading, Vermont.
68. Wallpaper stencil from house in Upton, Massachusetts.
69. Wall stencil, Mowry Tavern, Smithfield, Rhode Island.
70. Wall stencil, Thompson house, Alewive, Kennebunk, Maine, c. 1850.
71. Wall stencil, Ira Buel house, Milton, Connecticut.
72. Wall stencil, Jesse Ayre house, Hampstead, New Hampshire, c. 1800.
73. Wall stencil, Elisha Smith house, Stillwater, Rhode Island.
74–76. Wall stencil, Oliver Smith house, Tyringham, Massachusetts.
77. Wall stencil, Elisha Smith house, Stillwater, Rhode Island.
78. Wall stencil, Josiah Sage house, South Sandisfield, Massachusetts.
79. Appliqué quilt, variation of "Orange Peel" pattern, Damariscotta, Maine.
80. Wall stencil, Mowry Tavern, Smithfield, Rhode Island.
81. Stencil. *Metropolitan Museum of Art,* New York.
82–84. Wall stencils, William L. Gardiner house, Garfield, New York.
85. Stencil, "Pineapple" motif, by Moses Eaton, Grant House, North Saco, Maine.
86. Wall stencil, Slack house, Plymouth, Vermont.
87. Wall stencil, Mansel Alcock house, Hancock, New Hampshire.
88. Stencil, Josiah Sage house, South Sandisfield, Massachusetts.
89. Wall stencil, Elisha Smith house, Stillwater, Rhode Island.
90. Pennsylvania German two-handled jar, made by George Hubener, 1785–89. Collection Arthur J. Sussel.
91. Pennsylvania German plate, Bucks County, Pennsylvania, 1794.
92. Pennsylvania German sgraffito dish, 1810. *Philadelphia Museum of Art.*
93. Pennsylvania German sgraffito pie dish, c. 1800. *Philadelphia Museum of Art.*
94. Pennsylvania German sgraffito dish, 1805. *Metropolitan Museum of Art,* New York.
95. Painted Pennsylvania German dower chest.
96. Esther Bechtel's fraktur bookplate. Courtesy *The Rare Book Room, Philadelphia Free Library* and *The Pennsylvania German Society.*
97. Painted Pennsylvania German dower chest.
98. Pennsylvania German sgraffito and slip ware plate. Courtesy Mrs. Ralph Beaver Strassburger.
99. Painted Pennsylvania German chest made for Susana Ackerman, 1792.
100. Pennsylvania German fluted dish, sgraffito decoration, made by Samuel Troxel, dated 1823.

101. Catherine Guth's fraktur bookplate. Courtesy *The Rare Book Room, Philadelphia Free Library* and *The Pennsylvania German Society.*
102. Pennsylvania German fractur design.
103. Pennsylvania German dower chest painted by Christian Seltzer, Jonestown, Columbia County, dated 1784. Courtesy *Antiques.*
104. Fractur, 1797. Cassel Collection. *Historical Society of Pennsylvania,* Philadelphia.
105. Pennsylvania German sgraffito dish, tulip decoration, southeastern Pennsylvania, 1789.
106. Pennsylvania German earthenware plate with slip and sgraffito decoration, c. 1790. *Metropolitan Museum of Art,* New York.
107. Etched and enamelled white flint flip glass.
108. Etched and enamelled Stiegel flip glass.
109. Sgraffito plate.
110. Fractur from Pennsylvania German bookplate.
111. Pennsylvania German sgraffito plate. *Philadelphia Museum of Art.*
112. Pennsylvania German fractur drawing.
113. Pennsylvania German fractur drawing, the birth certificate of Henry Osborn. M. and M. Karolik Collection of American Water Colors and Drawings. *Museum of Fine Arts,* Boston.
114. Pennsylvania German sgraffito jar, c. 1800. *Philadelphia Museum of Art.*
115. Pennsylvania German fractur painting. M. and M. Karolik Collection of American Water Colors and Drawings. *Museum of Fine Arts,* Boston.
116. Etched and enamelled white flint flip glass.
117. Painted Pennsylvania German chest.
118, 119. Pennsylvania German red ware jar.
120. Painted Pennsylvania German dower chest.
121. Pennsylvania German sgraffito dish, Eastern Pennsylvania, 1762. *Philadelphia Museum of Art.*
122. Pennsylvania German fractur from the *Paradische-Wunderspiel,* Ephrata, 1754.
123. Large Pennsylvania German slip-decorated vegetable or meat dish. *Philadelphia Museum of Art.*
124. Pennsylvania German sgraffito dish, tulip decoration, made by John Leidy, 1796. *Philadelphia Museum of Art.*
125. Pennsylvania German sgraffito plate. *Brooklyn Museum.*
126. Pennsylvania German slip ware dish, tulip decoration, made by John Leidy, 1797. *Philadelphia Museum of Art.*
127. Pennsylvania German sgraffito jar made by Jacob Scholl, c. 1830.
128. Etched and enamelled white flint flip glass (motif reversed).
129. Slip painted dish, southeastern Pennsylvania, c. 1796. *Philadelphia Museum of Art.*
130. Pennsylvania German plate, tulip motif. *Philadelphia Museum of Art.*
131. Pennsylvania German plate, double-headed eagle decoration.
132. Pennsylvania German slip ware, sgraffito decoration. *Metropolitan Museum of Art,* New York.
133. Tulip stalk with two small birds, in pen and watercolor, Doylestown, Pennsylvania. M. and M. Karolik Collection of American Water Colors and Drawings. *Museum of Fine Arts,* Boston.

134. Painted chest made for Anne Beer.

135. Chest, late 18th century.

136. Pennsylvania German panel with branching stalk of tulips in pen and watercolor. M. and M. Karolik Collection of American Water Colors and Drawings. *Museum of Fine Arts*, Boston.

137. Painted Guilford Chest, Guilford, Connecticut, c. 1700.

138. Fractur from bookmark. Courtesy *The Rare Book Room, Philadelphia Free Library* and *The Pennsylvania German Society.*

139. Painted chest made for Anne Beer.

140. Painted bride's box.

141. Trinket box. *Metropolitan Museum of Art*, New York.

142. Slip ware barber's basin.

143. Painted chest, 1792.

144. Pennsylvania German slip ware, sgraffito decoration. *Metropolitan Museum of Art*, New York.

145. Pennsylvania German sgraffito plate, 1834. *Museum of Fine Arts*, Boston. Acc. No. 02.323.

146. Chest, Salem, Massachusetts, c. 1796. *Museum of Fine Arts*, Boston. Acc. No. 41.580.

147. Painted bellows, Vermont, early 19th century. Courtesy *Antiques.*

148–150. Chest, Salem, Massachusetts, c. 1796. *Museum of Fine Arts*, Boston. Acc. No. 41.580.

151. Chest, 1790.

152–158. Pennsylvania German cross-stitch towel. *Museum of Fine Arts*, Boston. Acc. No. 51.15.

159. Woven coverlet. *National Gallery of Art*, Washington.

160. Cross-stitch design from sampler.

161–163. Crewel embroidered curtain. *Museum of Fine Arts*, Boston. Acc. No. 42.390c.

164. Needlepoint chair seat. *Museum of Fine Arts*, Boston. Acc. No. 43.1331.

165. Embroidered chair seat, c. 1776. *Museum of Fine Arts*, Boston. Acc. No. 41.777.

166. Embroidered bed hangings, New England, 18th century. *Museum of Fine Arts*, Boston. Acc. No. 56.836.

167, 168. Crewel embroidered narrow bed curtain border, Ipswich, Massachusetts, 1720–50. *Museum of Fine Arts*, Boston. Acc. No. 57.472. Gift of Mrs. Jason Westerfield.

169. Crewel embroidered bed cover. *Museum of Fine Arts*, Boston. Acc. No. 19.67.

170, 171. Crewel embroidered curtain. *Museum of Fine Arts*, Boston. Acc. No. 42.390c.

172–174. "Candlewick" embroidered bedspread.

175. Crewel embroidered curtain. *Museum of Fine Arts*, Boston. Acc. No. 42.390c.

176, 177. Crewel embroidered curtain, *Museum of Fine Arts*, Boston.

178, 179. Crewel embroidered bed cover. *Museum of Fine Arts*, Boston. Acc. No. 19.67.

180, 181. Crewel embroidered curtain. *Museum of Fine Arts*, Boston. Acc. No. 42.390c and b.

182–191. Blue embroidered motifs on white linen. *Museum of Fine Arts*, Boston. Acc. No. 43.1504.

192. Crewel embroidered bed curtain, New England, 1700–50. *Museum of Fine Arts*, Boston. Acc. No. 19.67. Gift of Samuel Bradstreet.

193. Crewel embroidered petticoat border, New England, 18th century. *Museum of Fine Arts*, Boston. Acc. No. 19.609.

194, 195. Crewel embroidered bed curtain, New England, 1700–50. *Museum of Fine Arts*, Boston. Acc. No. 19.67. Gift of Samuel Bradstreet.

196. Motif from the "Sally Grant Coverlet." *Brooklyn Museum.*

197–199. Crewel embroidered bedspread, wool twill weave cotton. Courtesy *The Henry Francis du Pont Winterthur Museum*, Delaware. Acc. No. 60.597. Drawn from a photograph.

200. Embroidered linen seat cover, Connecticut, c. 1730. *Metropolitan Museum of Art*, New York. Gift of Mrs. J. Insley Blair, 1946. Drawn from a photograph.

201, 202. Crewel embroidered curtains. Gift of Mrs. Jason Westerfield. *Museum of Fine Arts*, Boston. Acc. No. 59.472a.

203. Crewel embroidered motif. *Museum of Fine Arts*, Boston. Acc. No. 40.717.

204. Needlepoint picture. *Museum of Fine Arts*, Boston. Acc. No. 41.6.

205. Crewel embroidered curtain. *Museum of Fine Arts*, Boston. Acc. No. 42.390c.

206. Embroidered linen seat cover, Connecticut, c. 1730. *Metropolitan Museum of Art*, New York. Gift of Mrs. J. Insley Blair. Drawn from a photograph.

207, 208. Crewel embroidered bedspread. Courtesy *The Henry Francis du pont Winterthur Museum*, Delaware. Acc. No. 60.597. Drawn from a photograph.

209. Embroidered bedspread in blue linen on white linen. *Museum of Fine Arts*, Boston. Acc. No. 50.4044.

210, 211. Crewel embroidered bedspread. Courtesy *The Henry Francis du Pont Winterthur Museum*, Delaware. Acc. No. 60.597. Drawn from a photograph.

212. Embroidered bedspread, 18th century. Courtesy *The Henry Francis du Pont Winterthur Museum*, Delaware. Drawn from a photograph.

213. Embroidered bedspread in blue linen on white linen. *Museum of Fine Arts*, Boston. Acc. No. 50.4044.

214. Embroidered clover design from a pocket.

215. Crewel embroidered valance. *Museum of Fine Arts*, Boston. Acc. No. 49.56.

216, 217. Embroidered bedspread in blue linen on white linen. *Museum of Fine Arts*, Boston. Acc. No. 50.4044.

218. Embroidered tulip design from a pocket.

219. Crewel embroidered bedspread. Courtesy *The Henry Francis du Pont Winterthur Museum*, Delaware. Acc. No. 60.597. Drawn from a photograph.

220–222. Embroidered bedspread in blue linen on white linen. *Museum of Fine Arts*, Boston. Acc. No. 50.4044.

223. Embroidered carnation from a pocket.

224, 225. Crewel embroidered bedspread, wool on twill weave cotton. Courtesy *The Henry Francis du Pont Winterthur Museum*, Delaware. Acc. No. 60.597. Drawn from a photograph.

226. Embroidered bed cover made by Lucinda Coleman. *Metropolitan Museum of Art*, New York. Sansbury Mills Fund, 1961.

227. Crewel embroidered bedspread. Courtesy *The Henry Francis du Pont Winterthur Museum*, Delaware. Acc. No. 60.597. Drawn from a photograph.

228. Crewel embroidered valance. *Museum of Fine Arts*, Boston. Acc. No. 49.1142.

229. Crewel embroidered chair seat. *Museum of Fine Arts*, Boston. Acc. No. 23.274.

230, 231. Embroidered bedspread, designed and made by Mary Breed, Boston, 1770.

232. Crewel embroidered chair seat. *Museum of Fine Arts*, Boston. Acc. No. 23.274.

233. Embroidered bedspread in blue linen on white linen. *Museum of Fine Arts*, Boston. Acc. No. 50.4044.

234. Crewel embroidered valance. *Museum of Fine Arts*, Boston. Acc. No. 32.64.

235. Crewel embroidered bedcurtain border, Ipswich Massachusetts, 1720–50. *Museum of Fine Arts*, Boston. Acc. No. 57.472. Gift of Mrs. Jason Westerfield.

236. Crewel embroidered bedspread. Courtesy *The Henry Francis du Pont Winterthur Museum*, Delaware. Acc. No. 60.597. Drawn from a photograph.

237. Crewel embroidered valance. *Museum of Fine Arts*, Boston. Acc. No. 32.64.

238. Embroidered bedspread in blue linen on white linen. *Museum of Fine Arts*, Boston. Acc. No. 50.4044.

239. Crewel embroidered valance. *Museum of Fine Arts*, Boston. Acc. No. 49.55.

240, 241. Crewel embroidered bed valance. *Museum of Fine Arts*, Boston. Acc. No. 49.1142.

242, 243. Crewel embroidered curtain. Gift of Mrs. Jason Westerfield. *Museum of Fine Arts*, Boston. Acc. No. 59.472a and b.

244. Crewel embroidered bed valance. *Museum of Fine Arts*, Boston. Acc. No. 49.1142.

245. Crewel embroidered motif. *Museum of Fine Arts*, Boston. Acc. No. 40.717.

246. Embroidered petticoat border. *Museum of Fine Arts*, Boston. Acc. No. 50.3175.

247. Embroidered bed curtain, wool on linen. Courtesy *The Henry Francis du Pont Winterthur Museum*, Delaware. Acc. No. 57.44.1 (a). Drawn from a photograph.

248, 249. Embroidered bedspread in blue linen on white linen. *Museum of Fine Arts*, Boston. Acc. No. 50.4044.

250, 251. Crewel embroidered border. *Museum of Fine Arts*, Boston. Acc. No. 50.3175.

252. Crewel embroidered bedspread in blue linen on white linen. *Museum of Fine Arts*, Boston. Acc. No. 50.4044.

253. Crewel embroidery by Mary Breed, 1770. *Metropolitan Museum of Art*, New York.

254, 255. Embroidered bedspread in blue linen on white linen. *Museum of Fine Arts*, Boston. Acc. No. 50.4044.

256. Molded slip ware dish, 1797. *Philadelphia Museum of Art*.

257. Appliqué quilt, York, Pennsylvania, c. 1850.

258. Pennsylvania German pie plate made by Fredrich Hildebrand, c. 1830.

259. Barber's basin, southeastern Pennsylvania, 1733.
260. Crewel embroidered valance. *Museum of Fine Arts*, Boston. Acc. No. 49.56.
261. Crewel embroidered bed curtain. Courtesy *The Henry Francis du Pont Winterthur Museum*, Delaware. Acc. No. 57.44.16. Drawn from a photograph.
262, 263. Crewel embroidered valance. *Museum of Fine Arts*, Boston. Acc. No. 49.56.
264. Embroidery from the "Sally Grant Coverlet." *Brooklyn Museum*.
265, 266. Crewel embroidered valance. *Museum of Fine Arts*, Boston. Acc. No. 49.55.
267. Crewel embroidery by Mary Breed, 1770. *Metropolitan Museum of Art*, New York.
268. Embroidered bed curtains, New England, 18th century. *Museum of Fine Arts*, Boston. Acc. No. 56.834.
269. Crewel embroidered curtain. Gift of Mrs. Jason Westerfield. *Museum of Fine Arts*, Boston. Acc. No. 59.472a.
270, 271. Crewel embroidered curtain. *Museum of Fine Arts*, Boston. Acc. No. 42.390c.
272, 273. Crewel embroidered curtain. Gift of Mrs. Jason Westerfield. *Museum of Fine Arts*, Boston. Acc. No. 59.472a and b.
274. Embroidered linen holder.
275, 276. Designs drawn and presumably embroidered by Elizabeth Hartwell of Edgartown, Massachusetts, 1786.
277. Crewel embroidered curtains, Gift of Mrs. Jason Westerfield. *Museum of Fine Arts*, Boston. Acc. No. 59.472b.
278. Crewel embroidered bedspread in blue linen on white linen. *Museum of Fine Arts*, Boston. Acc. No. 50.4044.
279. Crewel embroidered curtains. Gift of Mrs. Jason Westerfield. *Museum of Fine Arts*, Boston. Acc. No. 59.472a.
280. Fractur, Anna Stauffer's bookplate. Courtesy *The Rare Book Room, Philadelphia Free Library* and *the Pennsylvania German Society*.
281. Crewel embroidered bedspread in blue linen on white linen. *Museum of Fine Arts*, Boston. Acc. No. 50.4044.
282, 283. Crewel embroidered valance. *Museum of Fine Arts*, Boston. Acc. No. 49.1142.
284. Crewel embroidered valance. *Museum of Fine Arts*, Boston. Acc. No. 34.36.
285, 286. Crewel embroidered valance. *Museum of Fine Arts*, Boston. Acc. No. 49.1142.
287. Crewel embroidered border. *Museum of Fine Arts*, Boston, Acc. No. 50.3175.
288. Crewel embroidered valance. *Museum of Fine Arts*, Boston. Acc. No. 49.56.
289. Crewel embroidered valance. *Museum of Fine Arts*, Boston. Acc. No. 49.55.
290. Crewel embroidery, 18th century. *Museum of Fine Arts*, Boston. Acc. No. 61.405.
291. Crewel embroidered curtain. Gift of Mrs. Jason Westerfield. *Museum of Fine Arts*, Boston. Acc. No. 59.472a.
292. Crewel embroidered bed curtain, 1700–50. *Museum of Fine Arts*, Boston. Acc. No. 19.67.

293. Rose plant from crewel embroidered bed curtain, Ipswich, Massachusetts, 1720–50. *Museum of Fine Arts*, Boston. Acc. No. 59.473.

II. Landscapes

294–302. Embroidered petticoat border, Ipswich, Massachusetts, c. 1758. *Museum of Fine Arts*, Boston. Acc. No. 62.178.
303. Crewel embroidered curtain. *Museum of Fine Arts*, Boston. Acc. No. 42.390c.
304, 305. Embroidered linen seat cover, Connecticut, c. 1730. *Metropolitan Museum of Art*, New York. Gift of Mrs. J. Insley Blair, 1946. Drawn from a photograph.
306. Crewel embroidered bed valance. *Museum of Fine Arts*, Boston. Acc. No. 49.1142.
307. Appliqué quilt, "Cherry Tree and Birds" pattern, c. 1820.
308. Embroidered linen seat cover, Connecticut, c. 1730. *Metropolitan Museum of Art*, New York. Gift of Mrs. J. Insley Blair, 1946. Drawn from a photograph.
309. Crewel embroidered valance. *Museum of Fine Arts*, Boston. Acc. No. 49.56.
310. Embroidered valance. *Museum of Fine Arts*, Boston. Acc. No. 33.407.
311. Embroidered valance. *Museum of Fine Arts*, Boston. Acc. No. 49.1142.
312. Appliqué quilt, 19th century.
313–318. Embroidered valance. *Museum of Fine Arts*, Boston. Acc. No. 33.407.
319–321. Embroidered petticoat border, Ipswich, Massachusetts, c. 1758. *Museum of Fine Arts*, Boston. Acc. No. 62.178.
322. Crewel embroidered petticoat border, 1725–50. *Museum of Fine Arts*, Boston. Acc. No. 25.186.
323. Embroidered petticoat border. *Museum of Fine Arts*, Boston. Acc. No. 32.64.
324. Crewel embroidered chair seat. *Museum of Fine Arts*, Boston. Acc. No. 23.274.
325. Embroidered valance. *Museum of Fine Arts*, Boston. Acc. No. 33.407.
326. Stencil. *Metropolitan Museum of Art*, New York.
327. Embroidered chair seat. *Museum of Fine Arts*, Boston. Acc. No. 24.362.

III. Birds and Animals

328. Weather vane. *The New-York Historical Society*.
329. Peacock weather vane, copper painted gold. M. and M. Karolik Collection. *Museum of Fine Arts*, Boston. Cat. 1411.
330. Weather cock found in Montgomery County, Pennsylvania.
331. Appliqué bird motif.
332. Weather cock.
333. Weather cock from Berks County, Pennsylvania.
334. Weather vane from the spire of the Dutch Reformed Church, Albany, New York, 1656.
335. Sunflower plant and two birds, pen and watercolor. M. and M. Karolik Collection of American Water Colors and Drawings. *Museum of Fine Arts*, Boston.
336. Fractur drawing.

337. Stylized rooster carved in pine wood and polychromed, found in New York.

338. Embroidery in colored silks on fine cotton cloth. Collection Mr. Maurice Brix, Philadelphia.

339. Painted toy bird with glass eye.

340. Carved bird, stained and varnished, late 19th century.

341. Carved bird.

342. Fractur bird from birth certificate drawn by Daniel Peterman, Shrewsbury Township, York County, Pennsylvania.

343. Carved and painted bird from Berks County, Pennsylvania.

344. Crewel embroidered bed curtain. Courtesy *The Henry Francis du Pont Winterthur Museum,* Delaware. Acc. No. 57.44.lb. Drawn from a photograph.

345. Appliqué from "Album" or "Friendship" quilt.

346. Fractur valentine, 1787. Collection Arthur J. Sussel, Philadelphia.

347. Crewel embroidered bed curtain. Courtesy *The Henry Francis du Pont Winterthur Museum,* Delaware. Acc. No. 57.44.lb. Drawn from a photograph.

348. Woven coverlet. *National Gallery of Art,* Washington.

349. Pennsylvania German cross-stitch towel. *Museum of Fine Arts,* Boston. Acc. No. 51.15.

350. Fractur robin.

351. Sgraffito decoration, Pennsylvania German slip ware plate.

352. Pennsylvania German sgraffito pie plate with eagle decoration. *Philadelphia Museum of Art.*

353. Pennsylvania German sgraffito plate.

354. Sgraffito decoration, Pennsylvania German slip ware. *Metropolitan Museum of Art,* New York.

355. Two-handled jar made by George Hubener, 1785-89.

356. Sgraffito decoration, Pennsylvania German plate, by George Hubener, Montgomery County. Collection Mr. Burford Lorimer.

357. Pennsylvania German sgraffito plate.

358. Embroidery in colored silks on fine cotton cloth.

359. Painted diminutive chest.

360. Design from a Taunton chest painted by Robert Crosman, Taunton, Massachusetts, 1731. *Metropolitan Museum of Art,* New York.

361. Double-headed eagle motif from a Pennsylvania German sgraffito plate by George Hubener. *Philadelphia Museum of Art.*

362. Pennsylvania German slip ware pie dish made by Benjamin Bergey, Montgomery County, 1830. *Philadelphia Museum of Art.*

363. Fractur, bird on spray.

364. Fractur on birth certificate, Dauphin County, Pennsylvania, late 18th century. *Metropolitan Museum of Art,* New York.

365. Fractur drawing.

366. Painted chest.

367. Chest of drawers. *Philadelphia Museum of Art.*

368. Fractur.

369. Ceramic toy figures of cock and hen. *Philadelphia Museum of Art.*

370. Crewel embroidered curtain. *Museum of Fine Arts,* Boston. Acc. No. 42.390c.

371. Fractur drawing.

372. Small carved rooster with red comb. Collection Henry Kauffman.

373. Quilt, 1864.

374. Bird from birth certificate drawn by Daniel Peterman in Shrewsbury Township, York County, Pennsylvania.
375. Pennsylvania German sgraffito plate.
376. Punched tin design from door of Pennsylvania German pie safe.
377. Pennsylvania German plate, sgraffito decoration. *Philadelphia Museum of Art.*
378. Sgraffito plate.
379. Needlepoint picture. *Museum of Fine Arts*, Boston. Acc. No. 41.6.
380. Embroidered picture dated February 1733. *Museum of Fine Arts*, Boston. Acc. No. 42.556.
381. Crewel embroidered band, Vermont, late 18th century. *Museum of Fine Arts*, Boston. Acc. No. 38.79.
382. Embroidered picture dated February 1733. *Museum of Fine Arts*, Boston. Acc. No. 42.556.
383, 384. Needlepoint picture. *Museum of Fine Arts*, Boston. Acc. No. 46.1.
385. Embroidered picture dated February 1733. *Museum of Fine Arts*, Boston. Acc. No. 42.556.
386. Pennsylvania German earthenware plate, probably made by David Spinner, Bucks County, c. 1800. *Metropolitan Museum of Art*, New York.
387. Embroidered picture dated February 1733. *Museum of Fine Arts*, Boston. Acc. No. 42.556.
388. Needlepoint picture. *Museum of Fine Arts*, Boston. Acc. No. 41.6.
389. Crewel embroidered band, Vermont, late 18th century. *Museum of Fine Arts*, Boston. Acc. No. 38.79.
390. Needlepoint picture. *Museum of Fine Arts*, Boston. Acc. No. 41.6.
391. Needlepoint picture. *Museum of Fine Arts*, Boston. Acc. No. 41.559.
392. Needlepoint picture, *Museum of Fine Arts*, Boston. Acc. No. 41.6.
393. Slip ware dish. *Philadelphia Museum of Art.*
394–398. Needlepoint picture. *Museum of Fine Arts*, Boston. Acc. No. 41.6.
399. Embroidered picture. *Museum of Fine Arts*, Boston. Acc. No. 42.556.
400. Part of an embroidered border from an old colcha. Collection Mary C. Wheelwright.
401. Embroidered animal from an old colcha. Applegate Collection.
402, 403. Embroidered animals from an old colcha from Chamita, New Mexico.
404. Embroidered birds from the border of an old colcha. Collection Mary C. Wheelwright.
405. Embroidered bird from an old colcha.
406. Embroidered bird from the corner of an old colcha, Chamita, New Mexico.
407. Embroidered birds from the border of an old colcha. Collection Mary C. Wheelwright.

IV. BORDERS

408–411. Stencils. *Metropolitan Museum of Art*, New York.
412. Stencil. *Metropolitan Museum of Art*, New York.
413. Wall stencil by Moses Eaton, Grant house, North Saco, Maine.
414. Stencil. *Metropolitan Museum of Art*, New York.
415–418. Stencils. *Metropolitan Museum of Art*, New York.
419. Wall stencil, Belden house, New Boston, Massachusetts. Owned by Mrs. Goddard Du Bois.

420. Wall stencil, Mowry Tavern, Smithfield, Rhode Island.
421. Wall stencil by Moses Eaton, Grant house, North Saco, Maine.
422. Wall stencil, Barry House, Kennebunk, Maine, c. 1800.
423. Wall stencil, Mowry Tavern, Smithfield, Rhode Island.
424. Wall stencil, Robins house, Pittsfield, Massachusetts, c. 1800.
425. Stencil. *Metropolitan Museum of Art*, New York.
426. Wall stencil, Jesse Ayer house, Hampstead, New Hampshire.
427. Wall stencil, Elisha Smith house, Smithfield, Rhode Island.
428. Vine border, "Slashed Star" pattern, appliqué quilt, 1840.
429, 430. Appliqué quilt, "Lover's Knot" pattern, Maine, 1840.
431. Wall stencil, Josiah Sage house, South Sandisfield, Massachusetts.
432, 433. Pennsylvania German painted tray. *Metropolitan Museum of Art*, New York.
434. Stencil.
435. Stencil for chair rail.
436. Cornucopia from chest on chest. *Museum of Fine Arts*, Boston. Acc. No. 41.580.
437. Stencil.

V. MISCELLANEOUS

438–442. Cross-stitch alphabets from early American samplers.
443. Wall stencil, Ebenezer Robinson house, South Reading, Vermont. Owned by Mrs. H. M. Green.
444. Appliqué quilt, "Feathered Star" pattern.
445. Appliqué quilt, "Bear's Paw" pattern.
446. Appliqué quilt, "Sunrise" pattern.
447. Appliqué quilt, 1830.
448. Appliqué quilt, "Flower Basket" pattern, 1860.
449. Appliqué quilt.
450. Folded paper design for appliqué, 1820–30. *Landis Valley Museum*, Landis Valley, Pennsylvania.
451. Floor stencil, Connecticut, c. 1820.
452, 453. Units of early 19th-century standards.
454–456. Units of early 19th-century standards from Charlestown, South Carolina.
457. Section from gate, Paul Murphy house, French Quarter, New Orleans, Louisiana, 1803.
458, 459. Section of gate, Charlestown, South Carolina, probably 19th century.
460. Rail unit, Albany, New York.
461. Center from balcony, Charlestown, South Carolina.
462. Butterfly hinge, with leather washers under the nail heads which fasten it, Jabez Huntington house, Norwich, Connecticut, 1719.
463. Section of gate, Charlestown, South Carolina, probably early 19th century.
464. Butterfly hinge. Collection Mr. C. Musselman, Ephrata, Pennsylvania.
465. Rail unit, Albany, New York.
466. Hinges and hasp from a Conestoga wagon box. Collection Mr. Elmer D. Zimmerman, Monterey, Pennsylvania.
467. Iron hasp from Lancaster County, Pennsylvania.
468. Hinge and hasp of a Conestoga wagon tool box. *Philadelphia Museum of Art*.

469. Hasp and hinges of a Conestoga wagon box, flowering tulip design.
470. Pennsylvania German hinge, Moravian type with butterfly pintle brace, 1740. Collection Mr. Randolph R. Urich, Myerstown, Pennsylvania.
471. Cock's head hinge from a cupboard, Beckley house near Berlin, Connecticut.
472. Double L-hinge.
473. H and L extension hinge.
474. H and L hinge with decorated ends.
475. Strap hinge, William Judson house, Stratford, Connecticut, 1723.
476. Conestoga wagon box hinges and hasp with trident and tulip terminals.
477. Hasp with flaring tulip motif. Collection Mr. Randolph R. Urich, Myerstown, Pennsylvania.
478. Cock's head hinge, Ipswich, Massachusetts, 1665. Collection Mr. Ralph W. Burnham.
479. Hinge from a Conestoga wagon box. Owned by Mr. William B. Montague, Norristown, Pennsylvania.
480. Shutter bolt. Collection Mr. W. E. Irving, New York, New York.
481. Hasp with flaring tulip motif. Collection Mr. Randolph R. Urich, Myerstown, Pennsylvania.
482. Strap hinge. Owned by Mr. L. J. Gibert, Lebanon, Pennsylvania.
483. Strap hinge, Silliman house, Fairfield, Connecticut, 1760.
484. Strap hinge with tulip finials. Collection Randolph R. Urich, Myerstown, Pennsylvania.
485. Strap hinge with side member and tulip finial, Lancaster County, Pennsylvania.
486. Strap hinge, Capen house, Topsfield, Massachusetts, 1683.
487. Pennsylvania strap hinge, "Fleur-de-lis" type. *Junius Spencer Morgan Museum*, Hartford, Connecticut.
488. Strap hinge with tulip finial and bifurcated side member.
489. Strap hinge, "Fleur-de-lis" type, from an old house, Ulster County, New York.
490. Strap hinge, "Fleur-de-lis" type. *Bucks County Historical Society Museum*, Doylestown, Pennsylvania.
491. Strap hinge, "Fleur-de-lis" type.
492. Strap hinge with side members. Collection Mr. H. F. du Pont, Southampton, New York.
493. Strap hinge. Collection Mr. W. E. Bailey, Harrisburg, Pennsylvania.
494. Chest hinge from 17th-century chest belonging to Mrs. John D. McIlhenny. *Philadelphia Museum of Art.*
495. Pennsylvania chest offset hinge of tulip motif, Collection Mr. H. F. du Pont, Southampton, New York.
496. Chest hinge of tulip motif. Collection of Mr. William B. Montague, Norristown, Pennsylvania.
497. Pennsylvania chest hinge. Owned by Mrs. Charles Stauffert, Norristown, Pennsylvania.

BIBLIOGRAPHY

In compiling this book I have gone to several valuable books for inspiration and suggestion. These sources are given in the list of motifs that starts on page ix.

I am grateful to the publishers of the following volumes for their kind and understanding permission:

Mary Taylor Landon and Susan Brown Swan, *American Crewelwork*. The Macmillan Co., New York. Collier Macmillan Ltd., London, 1971.

Stearns, Martha G, *Homespun and Blue*. Bonanza Books, New York, 1963.

Davis, Mildred J., *Early American Embroidery Design*. Crown Publishers, Inc. New York, 1969.
          The Art of Crewel Embroidery, Crown Publishers, Inc. New York, 1962.

Barber, Edwin Atlee, *Tulip Ware of Pennsylvania-German Potters*. Dover Publications, Inc., New York, 1970.

          A Picture Book, Pennsylvania German Arts and Crafts, The Metropolitan Museum of Art, New York, 1949.

M. and M. Karolik Collection of American Watercolors and Drawings, 1800–1875, Vol. II. Museum of Fine Arts, Boston, 1962.

Lipman, Jean, *American Folk Decoration*, Dover Publications Inc., New York, 1972.

Stroudt, John Joseph, *Early Pennsylvania Arts and Crafts*. A. S. Barnes & Co., Inc., New York, 1964.

Robacher, Earl F., *Touch of the Dutchland*. A. S. Barnes & Co., Inc., New York and Thomas Yoseloff, Ltd., London.

Smith, Elmer L., *Antiques in Pennsylvania Dutchland*. Applied Arts Publishers, Lebanon, Pennsylvania.
          The Folk Art of Pennsylvania Dutchland. Applied Arts Publishers. Lebanon, Pennsylvania.

INDEX OF MOTIFS ACCORDING TO ORIGINAL USE

Figures refer to motif numbers. Letters refer to color plates, found between pages 12 and 13.

Appliqué, 4, 10, 11, 14, 16, 18, 19, 21–25, 27–29, 62, 63, 79, 257, 307, 312, 331, 345, 428–430, 444–449, G–J, L.

Ceramics, 90–94, 98, 100, 105, 106, 109, 111, 114, 118, 119, 121, 123–127, 129–132, 142, 144, 145, 256, 258, 351–357, 361, 362, 369, 375, 377, 378, 386, 393, D, N–Q.

Embroidery, 3, 6, 152–158, 160–255, 260–306, 308–311, 313–325, 327, 338, 344, 347, 349, 358, 370, 379–385, 387–392, 394–407, 438–442.

Etched and enamelled glass, 107, 108, 116, 128.

Fractur, 96, 101, 102, 104, 110, 112, 113, 115, 122, 138, 140, 336, 342, 346, 350, 363–365, 368, 371, 374.

Metalwork, 328–330, 332–334, 376, 452–497.

Painting on metal, 147, A.

Painting on wood, 95, 97, 99, 103, 117, 120, 134, 135, 137, 139–141, 143, 151, 359, 360, 366, 367, 432, 433, B, C, E, F.

Paper, 450.

Pen and watercolor, 133, 136, 335.

Quilting, 1, 2, 5, 7–9, 12, 13, 15, 17, 20, 26, 373.

Stenciling, 40–61, 64–78, 80–89, 326, 408–427, 431, 434, 435, 437, 443, 451.

Weaving, 159, 348, K, M.

Wood carving, 146, 148–150, 337, 339–341, 343, 372, 436.

1

2

1, 2 Quilting.

3 Embroidery. 4 Appliqué.

5

6

5 Quilting. 6 Embroidery.

7–9, 12 Quilting. 10, 11 Appliqué.

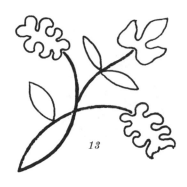

13

14

15

16

17

18

19

20

21

13, 15, 17, 20 Quilting. 14, 16, 18, 19, 21 Appliqué.

22–26 Appliqué.

40

41

40, 41 Stencils.

42

43

42, 43 Stencils.

44–48 Stencils.

49

50

51

49–51 Stencils.

52

53

52, 53 Stencils.

A. Toleware teapot.

B. Painted wooden box.

C. Painted wooden chest.

D. Earthenware plate.

E. Painted wooden chest.

F. Painted wooden panel.

G. Appliqué quilt.

H. Patchwork and appliqué quilt.

I. Appliqué quilted coverlet.

J. Appliqué quilt.

MADE • BY
J • WIRICK
IN ST • PARIS
CHAMPAIGN
CO. • OHIO •
1850 • FOR
CATHERINE
KINDIE

K. Woven coverlet.

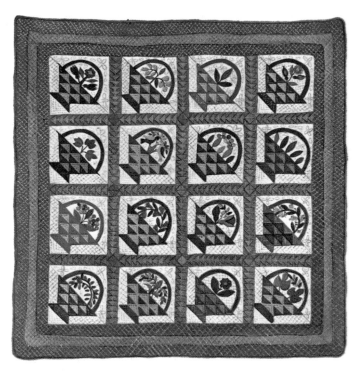

L. Patchwork and appliqué quilted bedspread.

M. Woven coverlet.

N. *Gray stoneware jar.*

O. *Gray stoneware jar.*

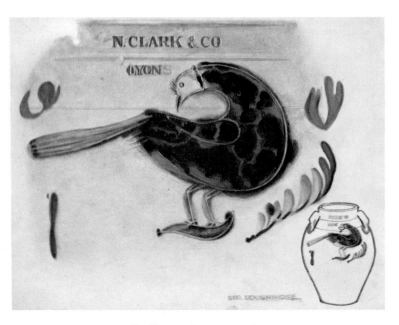

P. *Gray stoneware jar.*

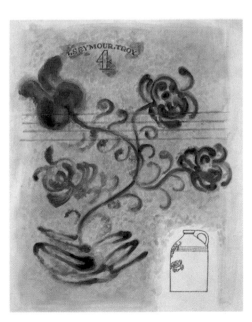

Q. *Gray stoneware jug.*

54–57 *Stencils.*

69

70

71

72

73

74

75

76

77

69–77 Stencils.

78, 80–89 Stencils. 79 Appliqué.

90

91

92

94

93

90–94 Ceramics.

95, 97 Painting on wood. 96 Fractur. 98 Ceramics.

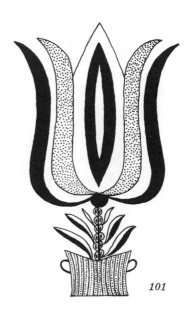

99 Painting on wood. 100 Ceramics. 101, 102 Fractur.

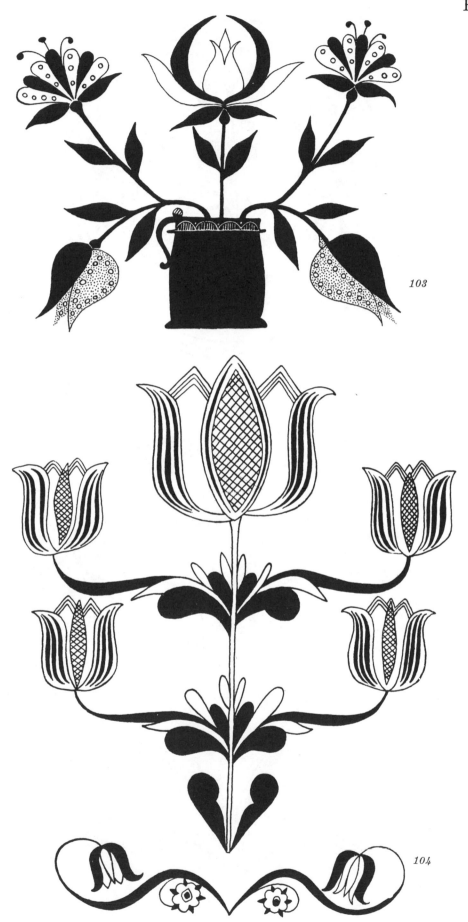

103

104

103 Painting on wood. 104 Fractur.

105

106

105, 106 Ceramics.

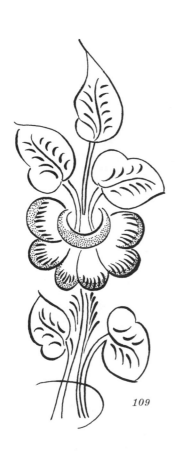

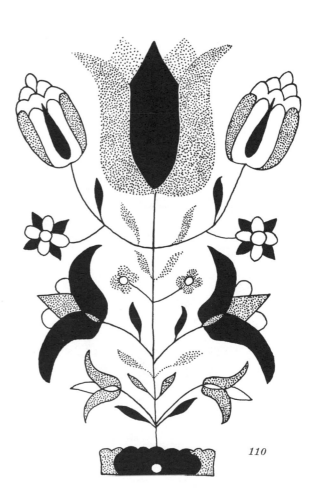

107, 108 Etched and enamelled glass. 109 Ceramics. 110 Fractur.

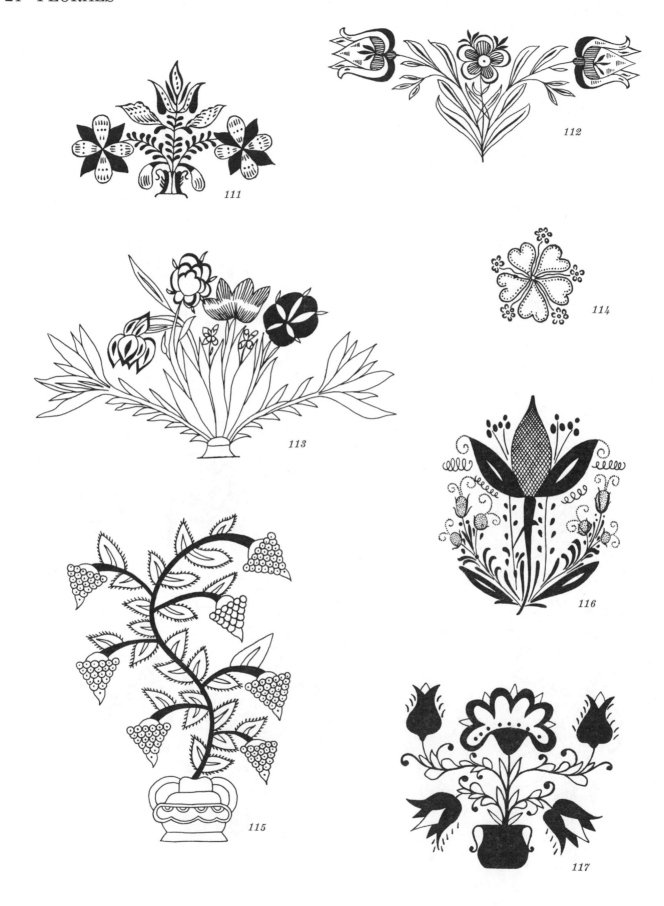

111, 114 Ceramics. 112, 113, 115 Fractur. 116 Etched and enamelled glass. 117 Painting on wood.

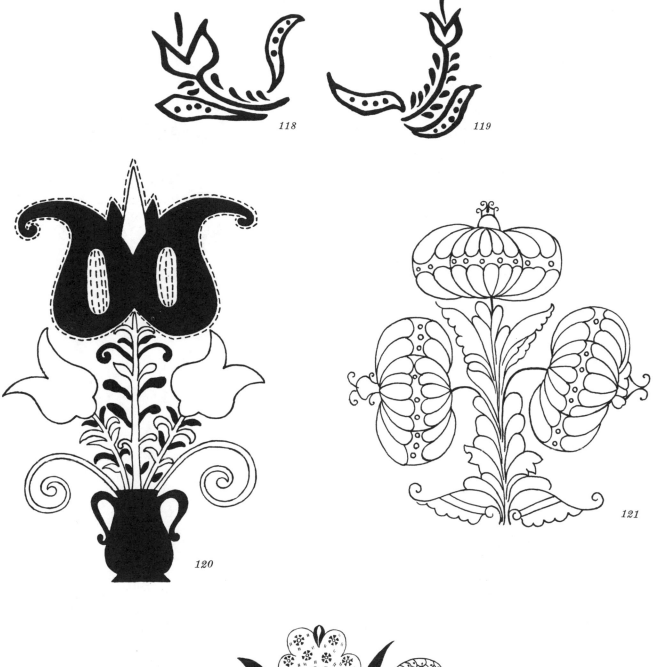

118, 119, 121 Ceramics. 120 Painting on wood. 122 Fractur.

123

124

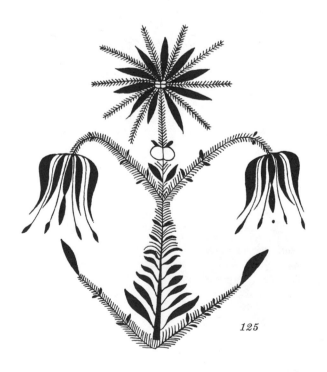

125

126

123–126 Ceramics.

127

128

129

130

131

132

127, 129–132 Ceramics. 128 Etched and enamelled glass.

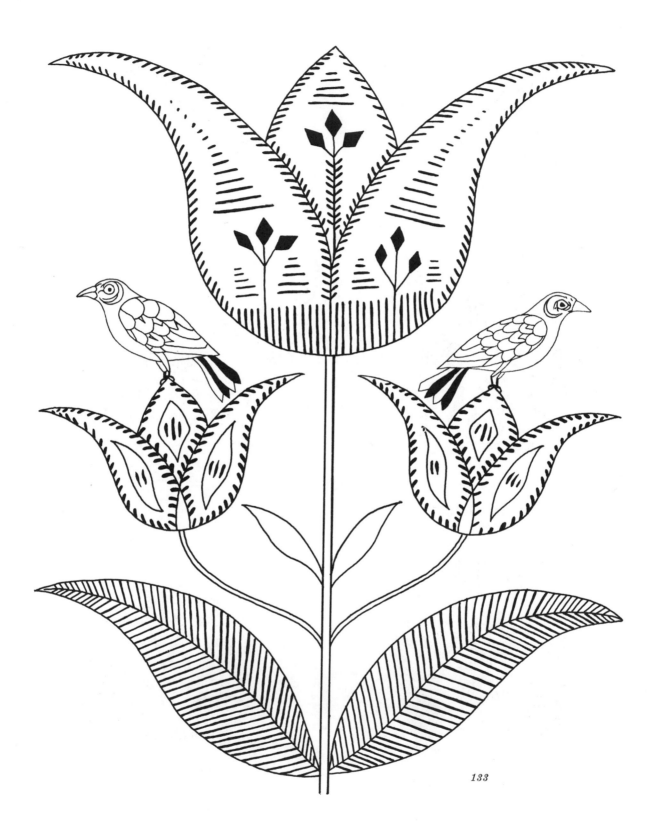

133

133 *Pen and watercolor.*

134, 135 *Painting on wood. 136 Pen and watercolor.*

137, 139, 141 Painting on wood. 138, 140 Fractur.

142, 144, 145 Ceramics. 143 Painting on wood.

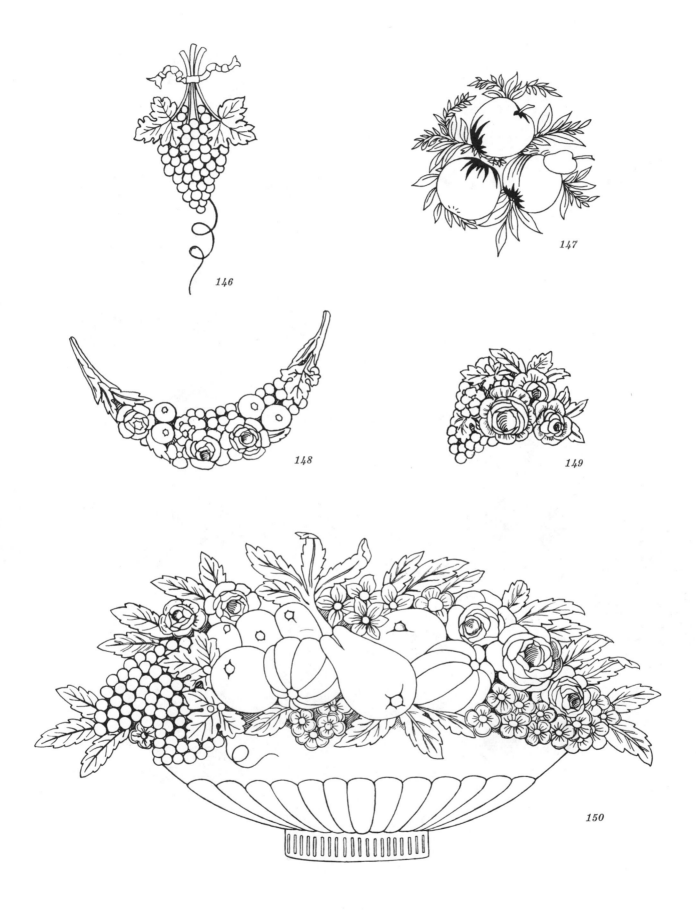

146, 148–150 Woodcarving. 147 Painting on metal.

151

151 *Painting on wood.*

152–154 *Embroidery.*

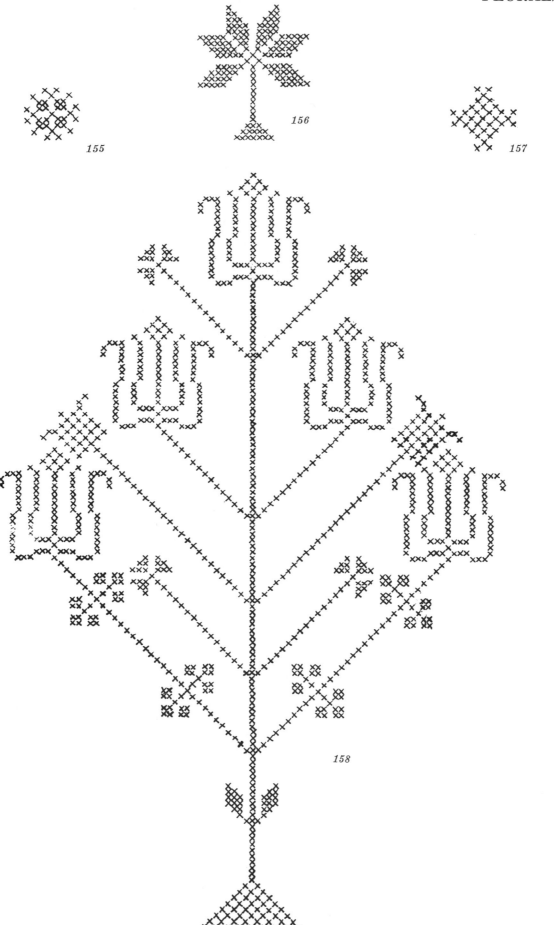

155–158 *Embroidery.*

159

160

159 Weaving. 160 Embroidery.

161

161 *Embroidery.*

162

162 Embroidery.

163

163 *Embroidery.*

165

165 *Embroidery.*

166

166 *Embroidery.*

167

168

167, 168 Embroidery.

169

169 *Embroidery.*

170

171

171 *Embroidery.*

172

173

174

172–174 *Embroidery.*

175

176

177

175–177 *Embroidery.*

178

179

178, 179 Embroidery.

180

181

180, 181 *Embroidery.*

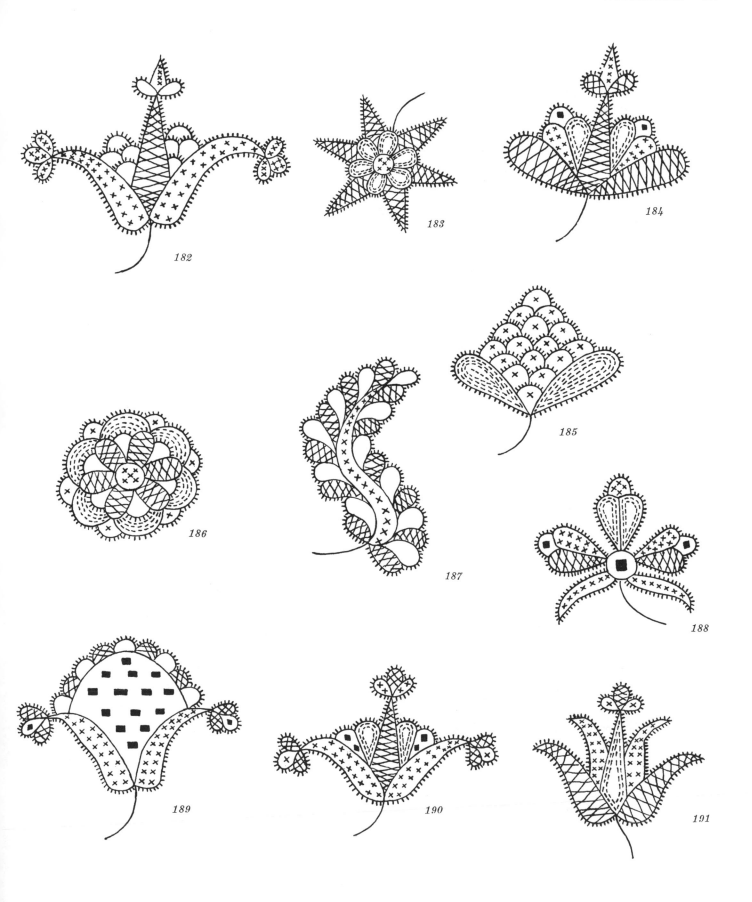

182–191 Embroidery.

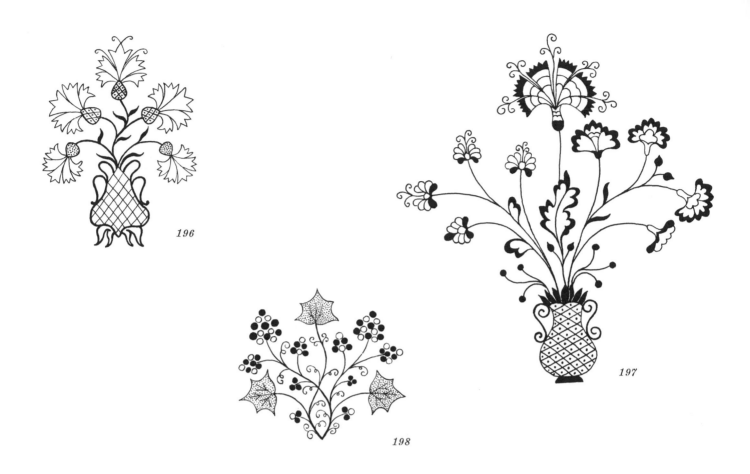

196–200 Embroidery.

201

202

203

204

205

206

201–206 *Embroidery.*

207

208

209

210

211

207–211 Embroidery.

212

213

214

215

216

217

218

219

220

212–220 Embroidery.

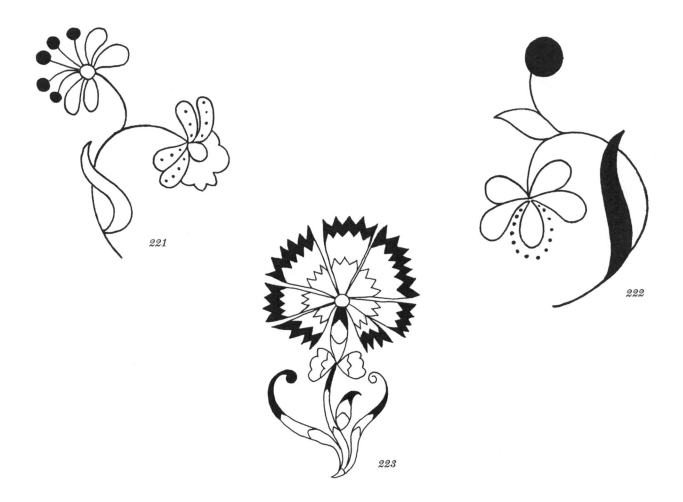

221–225 Embroidery.

226

227

228

229

230

231

226–231 *Embroidery.*

232–235 *Embroidery.*

236–239 *Embroidery.*

240–244 *Embroidery.*

245

246

247

245–247 Embroidery.

248

249

250

248–250 Embroidery.

251

252

253

251–253 *Embroidery.*

254

255

254, 255 Embroidery.

256 258

257

259

260

256, 258, 259 Ceramics. 257 Appliqué. 260 Embroidery.

261

262

263

261–263 Embroidery.

264

265

264, 265 Embroidery.

266

267

266, 267 Embroidery.

268, 269 Embroidery.

270

271

270, 271 Embroidery.

272

273

272, 273 Embroidery.

274

275

276

274–276 Embroidery.

277

278

279

277–279 Embroidery.

280

281

280 *Fractur.* 281 *Embroidery.*

282–284 *Embroidery.*

285

286

285, 286 Embroidery.

287

287 *Embroidery.*

288

289

288, 289 Embroidery.

290

290 Embroidery.

291

292

292 *Embroidery.*

293

294

294 *Embroidery.*

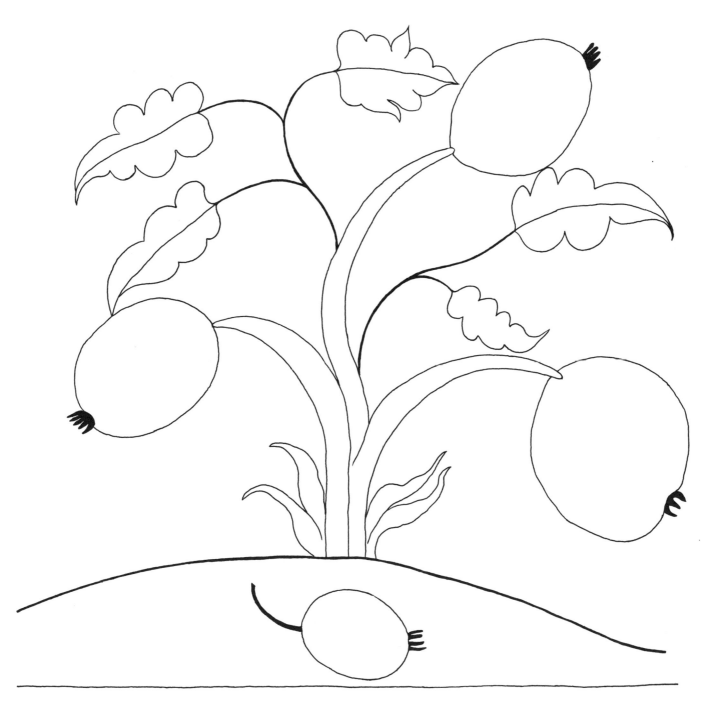

295

296

296 *Embroidery.*

297

297 Embroidery.

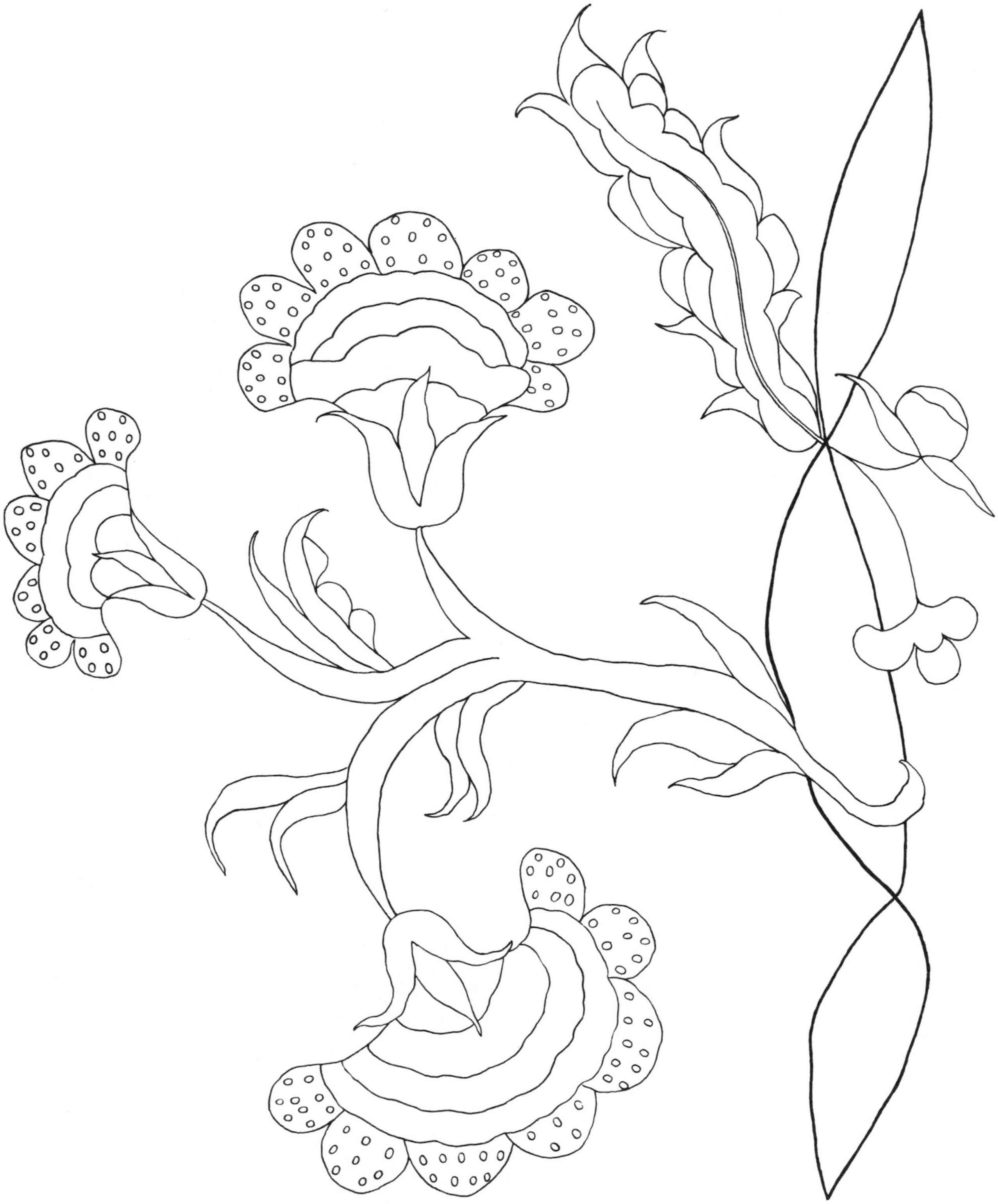

298

298 Embroidery.

299

300

300 Embroidery.

301

301 *Embroidery.*

302 Embroidery.

303

303 Embroidery.

304

305

304, 305 Embroidery.

306, 308 Embroidery. 307 Appliqué.

309–311 Embroidery. 312 Appliqué.

313–318 Embroidery.

319

320

320 Embroidery.

321

322 Embroidery.

323–325 Embroidery. 326 Stencil.

327

327 Embroidery.

328

329

328, 329 Metalwork.

330, 332–334 Metalwork. 331 Appliqué.

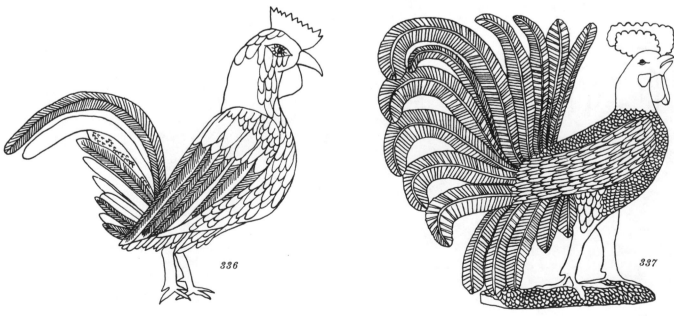

335 Pen and watercolor. 336 Fractur. 337 Woodcarving.

338 Embroidery. 339–341, 343 Woodcarving. 342 Fractur.

344 Embroidery. 345 Appliqué.

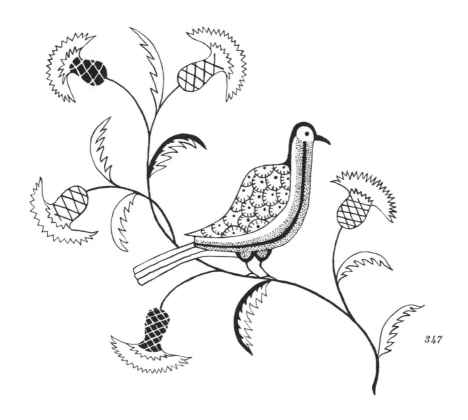

346 Fractur. 347 Embroidery.

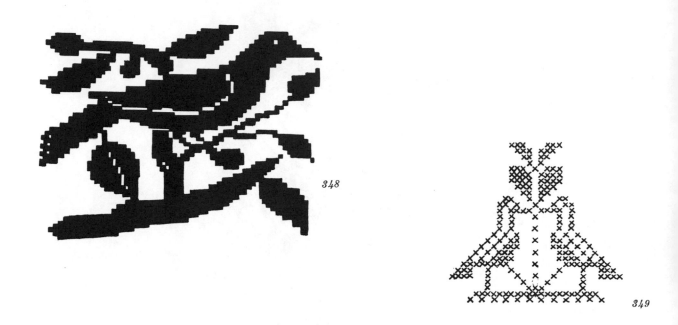

348 Weaving. 349 Embroidery. 350 Fractur.

351–353 Ceramics.

354–357 Ceramics.

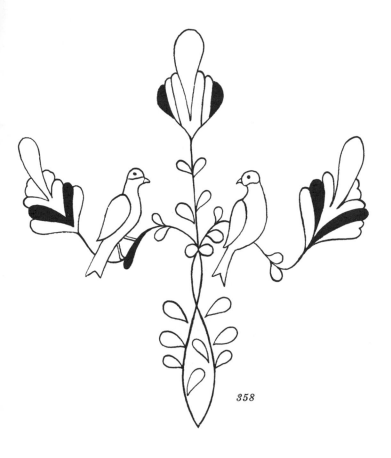

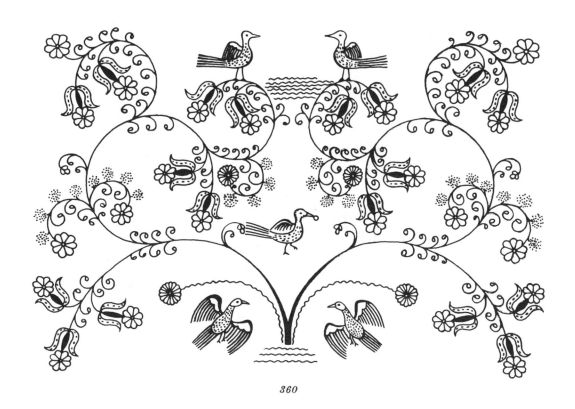

358 Embroidery. 359, 360 Painting on wood.

361, 362 Ceramics. 363 Fractur.

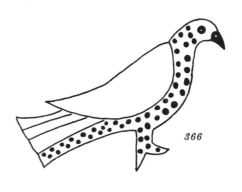

364, 365 Fractur. 366, 367 Painting on wood.

368 Fractur. 369 Ceramics. 370 Embroidery.

371, 374 Fractur. 372 Woodcarving. 373 Quilting. 375, 377, 378 Ceramics. 376 Metalwork.

379–385, 387–390 Embroidery. 386 Ceramics.

391, 392, 394–399 Embroidery. 393 Ceramics.

400–403 Embroidery.

404–407 *Embroidery.*

408

409

410

411

408–411 Stencils.

412

413

414

412–414 Stencils.

415

416

417

418

415–418 Stencils.

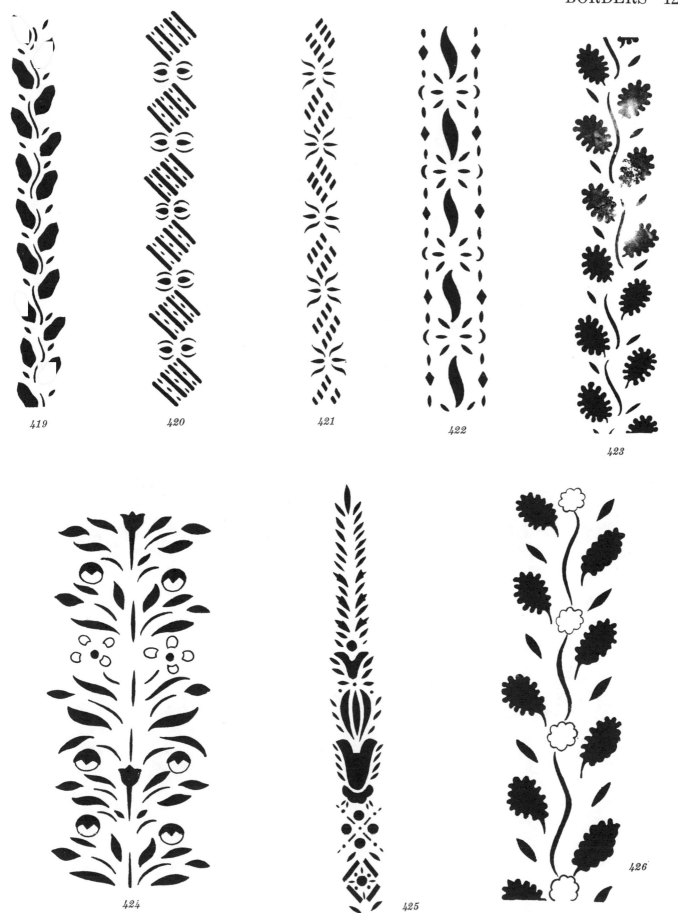

419   420   421   422   423

424   425   426

419–426 Stencils.

427

428

429

430

431

427, 431 Stencils   '0 Appliqué.

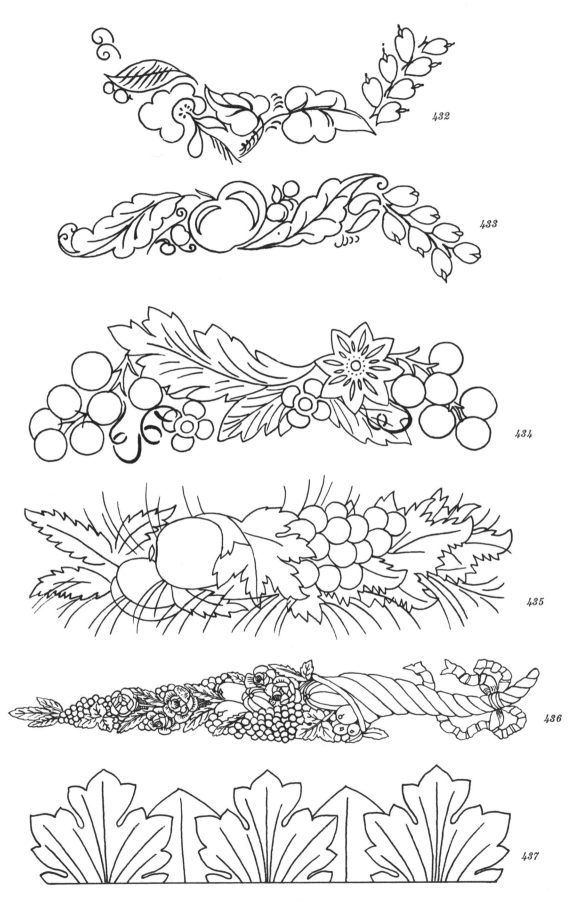

432, 433, Painting on wood. 434, 435, 437 Stencils. 436 Woodcarving.

438

439

438, 439 *Embroidery.*

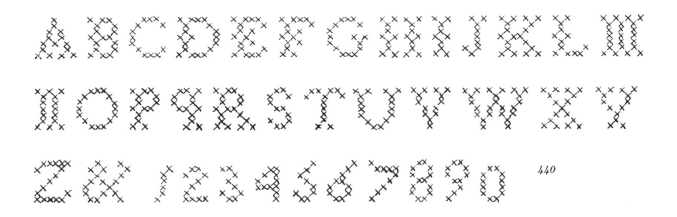

440, 441 Embroidery.

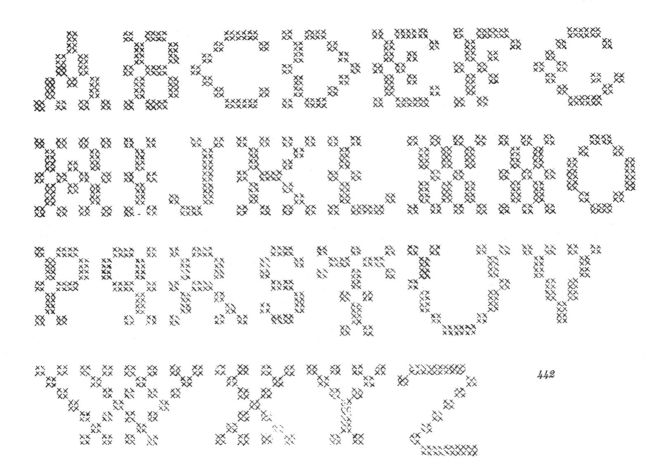

442 Embroidery.

443

444

445

446

447

448

449

443. *Stencil.* 444–449 *Appliqué.*

450

451

450 Paper. 451 Stencil.

452–465 Metalwork.

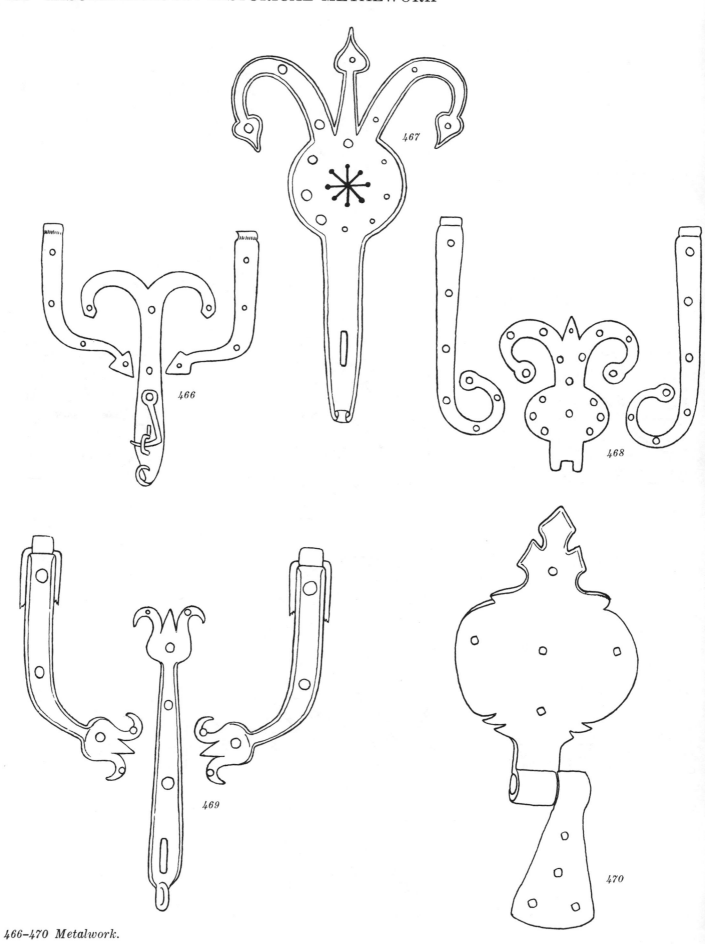

466–470 Metalwork.

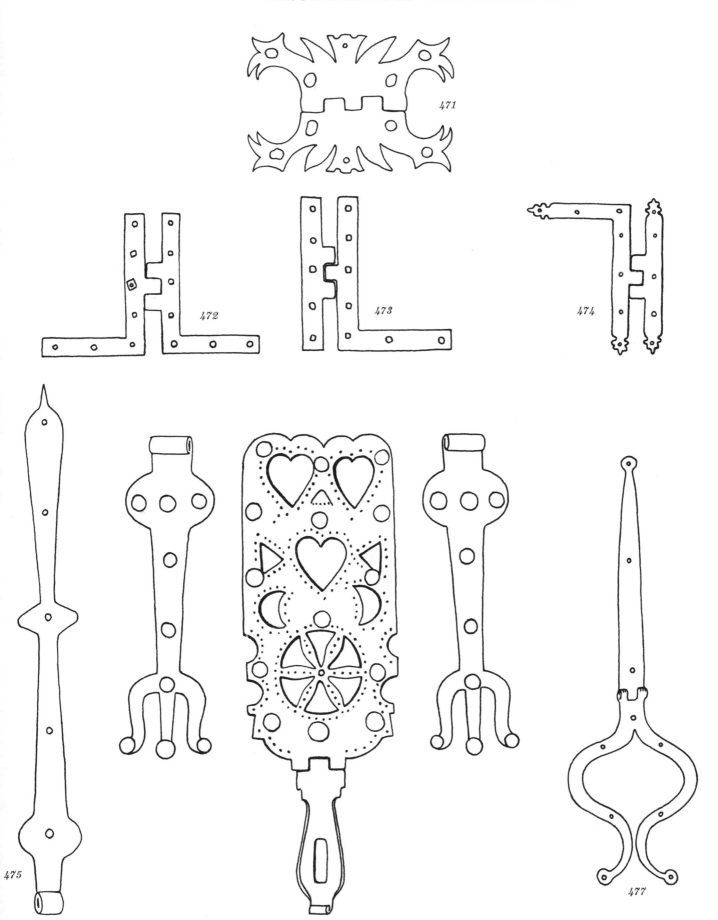

471–477 *Metalwork.*

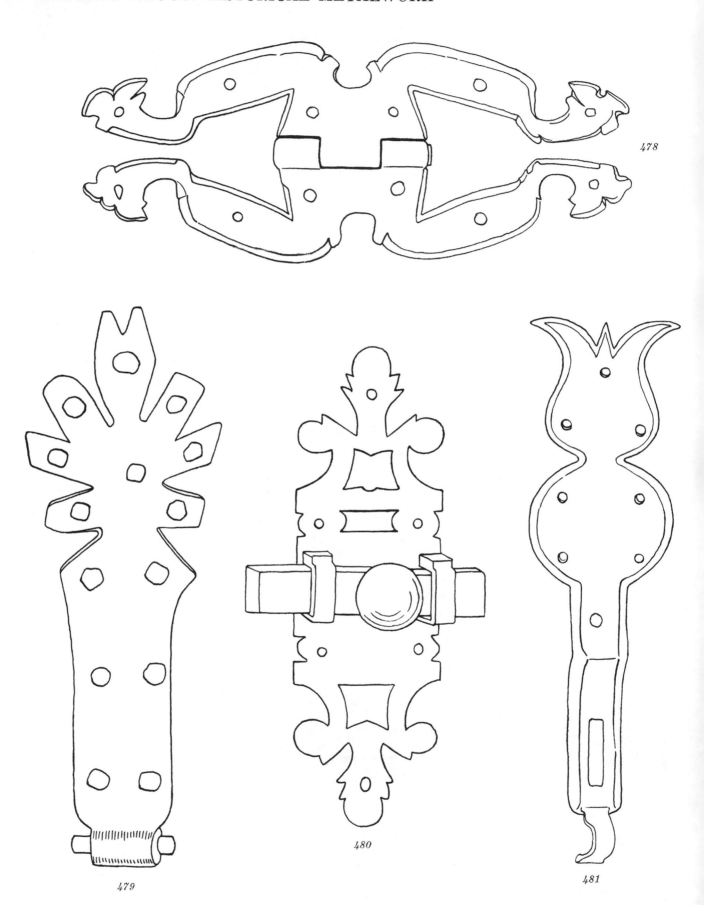

478

479

480

481

478–481 Metalwork.

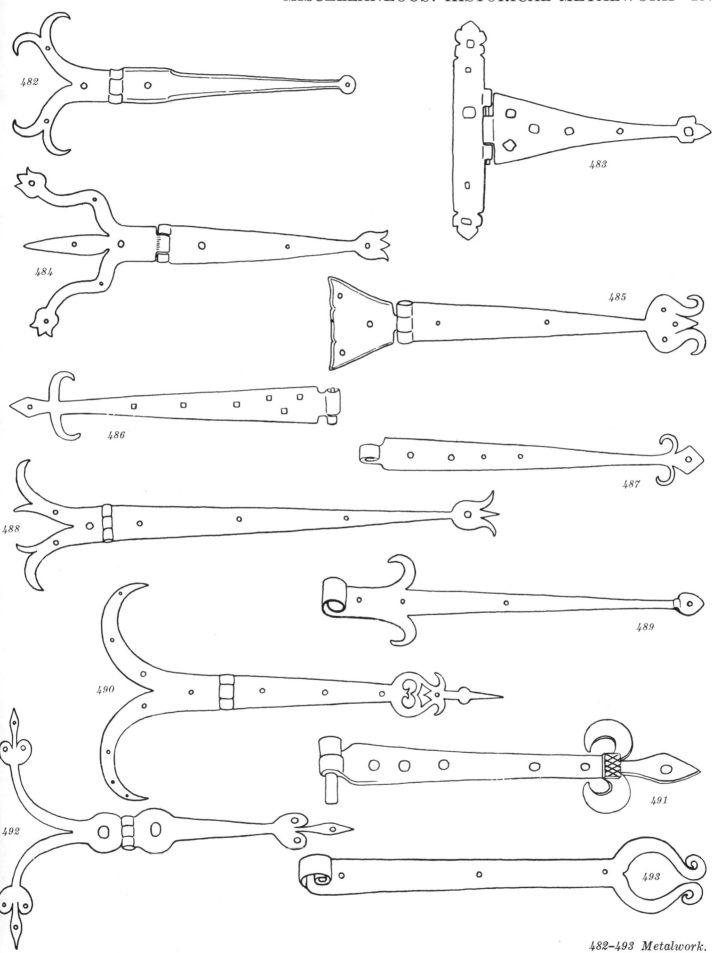

482–493 *Metalwork.*

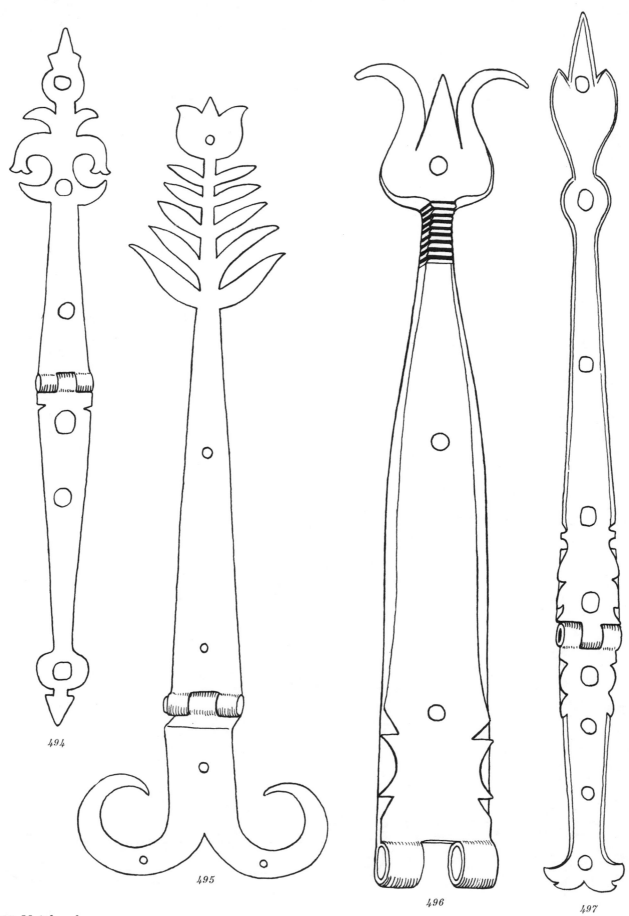

494

495

496

497

494-497 Metalwork.